CW00499806

PRAYI
REFORMERS

PRAYERS OF THE REFORMERS

THOMAS McPHERSON

MONARCH
BOOKS

Published by Monarch Books
an imprint of
Lion Hudson IP Ltd
Wilkinson House, Jordan Hill Road,
Oxford OX2 8DR, England

Email: monarch@lionhudson.com
www.lionhudson.com/monarch

ISBN 978 0 85721 880 3
e-ISBN 978 0 85721 882 7

First edition 2017

A catalogue record for this book is available from the British Library

Printed and bound in Great Britain by Marston Book Services Ltd, Oxfordshire

Prayer ought to be frequent and fervent.

—MARTIN LUTHER

No prayer is genuine which does not spring from faith,
and that comes by the Word of God.

—JOHN CALVIN

INTRODUCTION

Some historical events have such a profound impact and such a multitude of consequences that the world is changed forever in their wake. The Protestant Reformation must certainly be counted among such events. Given the loud repercussions—social, theological, cultural, liturgical (among so many others)—that have continued to echo through the centuries, even to our own day, it might be easy to forget that behind the forces that brought about such change were devout people of faith, whose everyday lives were marked by times of prayer. The Protestant "reformers," as they have come to be known, were also, and perhaps most importantly, "pray-ers." Certainly we learn much from the writings they have left, as well as the many records of their lives. But they have also left us their prayers, like windows into their own souls, and in their prayers we can meet them and learn from them.

The prayers of the Protestant Reformers are filled with some of the central themes of their faith, perhaps first among them being an unshakable confidence in *God's supreme authority* over all time and space. History is God's workplace. He does not stand afar off, but actively and intimately participates in the lives of people in order to show his love and bring about his will. Many of the Reformers' prayers reflect this conviction as, again and again, they seek for God's will to be done on earth, and in themselves. Asking for the grace to be obedient to God is not so much an expression of servility as it is an expression of hope—the hope that my ordinary life can play a part in God's extraordinary plan. The Reformers were convinced that we are all God's instruments for the working of his purposes, and so we pray for what we need in order to serve him faithfully.

A second recurring theme follows directly: *utter dependence on God* for everything needed to live for God. Here are prayers for wisdom, guidance, perseverance, protection, and for daily bread in all its forms, offered in the certainty that God alone is the source of such gifts. Turning to God with confidence starts by acknowledging one's own weakness and helplessness, beginning with the confession of one's own sin. Our dependence on God is never more profoundly apparent than when we stand (or fall) in need of his grace, mercy, and forgiveness, all of which are generously given through the shed blood of his only Son. For the Reformers, every prayer we offer is built upon the foundation of Christ's saving Cross and Resurrection.

Third, implicitly and sometimes explicitly, these prayers express our need for *illumination by the Holy Spirit and the Word of God*. In the writings of the Reformers there often appears an almost seamless movement between quotations from the Bible and phrases of prayer. As students of God's word, they conversed with God using his own "language." They believed that one must pray in order to understand the Scriptures, and that one must read the Scriptures in order to know how to pray. And, in both cases—when reading the Bible and when praying—they taught that we depend upon the Holy Spirit to shed God's light upon minds and hearts that would otherwise be left blind to God's handiwork. Praying for light is as important as praying for bread, for the Christian cannot live without either.

Fourth, *trust in God* stands as the chief motivator for prayer. Just as he is all-powerful, God is also all-loving. We express our needs and desires, sometimes cheerfully and sometimes despairingly, but always believing that God's answers will spring from an eternal love that is as unchangeable as it is mysterious. We ask *of* God because we trust *in* God, that he is faithful to his promises, that he is always ready to hear and to answer, and that he never will turn away when we call out to him. All of the Reformers expressed this kind of trust through their prayers, and some of them showed it even in the moment of their violent deaths.

Finally, for the Reformers, the ultimate goal of praying was the same as it was for living—*that God may be glorified.* Thanksgiving for God's goodness is directed to the same end as asking for God's forgiveness. In both cases, and in every case between, God's answer will elicit praise from our hearts as well as from our lips. If our aim is to live "to the praise of his glory," then woven through all of our prayers is the ultimate hope that, in Christ, God will unite all things in heaven and on earth, including us, into his everlasting kingdom. So we pray in order that his kingdom may come *now*, in whatever way it can, and that we will always be part of that coming.

This small volume of one hundred prayers, drawn from twelve Protestant Reformers, and spanning just over 300 years of history, is offered not as a textbook but as a tool. Of course, there is a good deal of distance between the language of fourteenth-century England or sixteenth-century Germany and our own day. To make them more useful aides to our own prayer, these have been excerpted, abridged, modernized, individualized (in most cases), titled, and lined out in phrases. Recalling the intimate connection made by the Reformers between prayer and Scripture, a Bible reference is also included with each prayer. Every effort has been made to remain faithful to each prayer's intent and meaning, while "translating" it for modern use. It is offered in observance of the five-hundredth anniversary of the Protestant Reformation, a reformation that, to make any lasting sounds at all, must continue to be voiced in hearts and words of prayer.

THE WRITERS OF THESE PRAYERS

JOHN WYCLIFFE (1320–1384)

Wycliffe was an English philosopher, theologian, pastor, and preacher. He maintained that the Bible was the sole criterion of doctrine, and this led him to challenge the authority of the pope and some of the prevailing teachings on the Eucharist and to call for a complete reform of the church in England. Wycliffe, whose views were condemned by the Church, was the inspiration for a translation of the Bible into English which was undertaken by his followers after his death.

JOHN HUS (1369–1415)

A Czech priest and well-known preacher in Prague, Hus was deeply influenced by Wycliffe, whose teachings at the time were widespread through Bohemia. When the tide turned against such calls for reform, Hus was silenced, excommunicated, and expelled from Prague, and his followers were placed under interdict. He was ultimately tried for heresy, condemned, and burned at the stake on July 6, 1415.

ULRICH ZWINGLI (1484–1531)

Zwingli was a Swiss priest and pastor, a devoted admirer of the humanist teachings of Erasmus, and a zealous student of Scripture (he taught himself Greek and learned the letters of Paul by heart). In Zurich he was made "People's Preacher," calling for political and religious reform in the church. The city council gave Zwingli its full support. Outside forces, however, led to armed conflict, and Zwingli, while serving as chaplain, was killed on the battlefield on October 11, 1531.

WILLIAM TYNDALE (1494–1536)

A student at both Oxford and Cambridge, in 1522 Tyndale conceived the idea of translating the Bible into English. Opposition was strong, however, so he left for Germany to undertake the project. He never returned to England. Though he never completed the Bible, his translations, made directly from Greek and Hebrew, became the basis for later English versions. The work remained highly controversial, however, and in 1535 he was arrested and later burned at the stake.

MARTIN LUTHER (1483–1546)

Considered the founder of the German Reformation, Luther began his religious career as a priest and Augustinian monk. As a doctor of theology and professor of biblical studies, he developed (and experienced) a doctrine of justification by faith that stood in opposition to the teaching of the church. The 95 theses on indulgences that he posted on the door of the church in Wittenberg eventually led to a massive movement of reform. He was a prolific writer of books, treatises, pamphlets, and hymns for disseminating the ideas of the Reformation.

MARTIN BUCER (1491–1551)

Bucer was a Dominican friar who, in Heidelberg, heard Martin Luther argue his positions for reform. He was dispensed from his vows, married, and began publicly to preach Lutheran doctrine. Some of his own teachings eventually departed from Luther's. After failed efforts at reconciliation between Protestants and Catholics, at the invitation of Thomas Cranmer he moved to England. There he was made Professor of Divinity at Cambridge, where he left a marked influence on parts of the Anglican rites for ordination.

THOMAS CRANMER (1489–1556)

Cranmer played an active role in supporting Henry VIII's divorce proceedings against Catherine of Aragon. In return, the King arranged for Cranmer's election as Archbishop of Canterbury in 1533. In that position, he became the chief instrument for renouncing the pope's authority over the Church of England. After Henry's death, under Edward VI Cranmer revised all church liturgies into the English language, composing the largely scripturally based 1549 *Book of Common Prayer*. Caught in the political forces of the successive monarchies, Cranmer was tried for heresy and burned at the stake on March 21, 1556.

PHILIP MELANCHTHON (1497–1560)

Melanchthon was professor of Greek at Wittenberg, Germany, where he interacted with Martin Luther, each influencing the other. When Luther was under house arrest in Wartburg, Melanchthon found himself head of the reformation movement. In his openness to some Catholic, Anabaptist, and Calvinist positions, he distanced himself somewhat though never separated himself from Lutheran doctrines. He was the chief architect of the Augsburg Confession of 1530 and later worked fervently for reconciliation between the Catholic and Lutheran churches.

JOHN CALVIN (1509–1564)

Calvin was a French theologian and pastor. He became familiar with the ideas of humanism and of Martin Luther while studying civil law. His growing sympathy with the Reformation movement forced him to leave France in 1535.

He was persuaded to come to Geneva to assist in organizing the Reformation there, but left for Strasbourg two years later at the invitation of Martin Bucer. After serving three years as pastor in that city (where he also produced an enlarged edition of his *Institutes*) he returned to Geneva, where he spent the next fourteen years establishing a church and civil society according to Reformation principles.

JOHN KNOX (1513–1572)

Knox was a Scottish Reformer whose early work as a private teacher came under the influence of continental reformers. Ordained a preacher in Glasgow, he was taken prisoner by the French, released, and eventually became chaplain to Edward VI of England and assisted in the revision of the prayer book of 1551. In 1553 he met John Calvin before returning to Scotland, where his preaching and writing met with great success. Finally, after some time serving the English Church in Geneva, he spent the rest of his life working to establish the Reformation in Scotland.

THEODORE BEZA (1519–1605)

The young Beza first began to take in the teachings of the Protestant Reformation under the tutelage of the famous German teacher Melchior Wolmar, who, for a brief time, also taught John Calvin. In 1548 Beza officially renounced his Catholic religion and went to Geneva, where Calvin eventually offered him a professorship at his newly founded academy, a post that Beza held until 1595. On the death of Calvin in 1564, Beza became the official head of the Calvinist movement in Europe.

LANCELOT ANDREWES (1555–1626)

A masterful preacher, a devoted scholar and master of 15 languages, Andrewes attracted the attention of Elizabeth I and became Dean of Westminster. Under James I he was made Bishop of Chichester, then of Ely, and finally of Winchester in 1619. He was an official translator of the Authorized Version of the Bible (known also as the King James Version). His collection of devotions, *Private Prayers*, though compiled for private use, was eventually published and broadly spread.

— JOHN WYCLIFFE —

1. *Lord, give me grace*

JAMES 3:17

Lord, give me grace to hold righteousness in all things,
that I may lead a clean and blessed life, and wisely flee evil.
Help me to understand the treacherous deceit of the devil,
so that I may not be fooled by any of his lies.
Make me mild, peaceable, considerate, and self-controlled,
so that I may act sincerely for the good of others.
And make me steadfast and strong.
Finally, Lord, let me be quiet in words,
so that I may not speak foolishly, but only what is appropriate.
  Amen.

2. *For my conversion*

JEREMIAH 17:14

Lord Jesus, turn me toward you,
so that I may be completely yours.
Heal me, so that I may be completely whole.
Without your grace and help
I can never be truly yours,
nor truly whole. Amen.

3. *Lord, stay with me*

LUKE 24:29

My Lord, from here on never leave me, but stay and dwell
   with me;
for your presence is my only comfort and consolation,
just as your absence is my only sorrow.
O Holy Spirit, come into my heart,
and draw me so near to God, that the things of the world
   may be as nothing to me.
Inflame my heart with your love,
and there let it burn without ceasing.
Come, I pray, for you are my true joy,
my only desire,
and my sweetest love. Amen.

4. *For my enemies*

LUKE 23:34

Lord Jesus Christ, I commit my soul into your hands,

for you have redeemed me with your blood.

Father in Heaven, do not hold against my enemies the sins
they commit against me;

rather, let me know that they will be at peace in your
presence.

O Holy Spirit, enlighten their hearts,

so that the truth of the Gospel may open their eyes,

and its praise may be spread everywhere,

forever and ever. Amen.

5. *For faith and courage*

2 CORINTHIANS 12:10

O loving Christ, draw me, weak as I am, to your side,
for if you do not draw me, I can never follow you.
Give me a brave spirit, so that it may always stand ready and
  strong.
And when my flesh is weak,
let your grace go before me,
come beside me,
and follow after me,
for without you, I can do nothing—least of all suffer pain or
  death.
Grant me a fearless heart,
a true faith,
a firm hope,
and a perfect love,
so that for your sake I may lay down my life with patience
  and joy. Amen.

ULRICH ZWINGLI

6. *For the light of God's word*

PSALM 119:105

Almighty, eternal, and merciful God,

whose Word is a lamp to my feet and a light to my path,

open and illuminate my mind, that I may truly understand
   your Word

and that my life may be conformed to what I have rightly
   understood,

that in all my ways I may be pleasing to you,

through Jesus Christ our Lord. Amen.

7. *In a time of great suffering*

PSALM 23:4

(The following was written by Zwingli while the Black Death broke out in Zurich in 1519)

Help me, O Lord,
  My strength and rock;
  Lo, at the door
  I hear death's knock
Lift up your arm,
  Once pierced for me,
  That conquered death,
  And set me free.
Yet, if your voice,
  In life's midday
  Recalls my soul,
  Then I obey.
In faith and hope
  I give up earth.
  Secure of heaven,
  My life's true birth.
My pains increase;
  Haste to console;
  For fear and woe
  Seize body and soul.
Death is at hand.

My senses fail.
My tongue is still;
Now, Christ, prevail.
Lo! Satan strains
To snatch his prey;
I feel his grasp;
Must I give way?
He harms me not,
I fear no loss,
For here I lie
Beneath your cross.
My God! My Lord!
Healed by your hand,
Upon the earth
Once more I stand.
Sin, no more,
My soul can own.
My mouth shall sing
To you alone.
Though now delayed,
My hour will come,
Involved, perhaps,
In deeper gloom.
But, let it come;
With joy I'll rise,
And bear my yoke
Straight to the skies.

8. *In a time of illness*

PSALM 6:2

(1519 – This prayer was written during a serious illness.)

Console me, Lord God, console me!
The illness increases,
Pain and fear seize
My soul and body.
Come to me then,
With your grace, O my only consolation!
It will surely save
Everyone, who
Sets his Heart's desire
And hope on you,
And who, besides,
Despises all gain and loss.
Now all is up,
My tongue is dumb,
It cannot speak a word.
My senses are all blighted.
Therefore, is it time
For you to conduct my fight,

From here on,
Since I am not
So strong, that I
Can bravely
Make resistance
To the Devil's wiles and treacherous hand?
Still will my spirit
Constantly abide by you, however he rages.

— WILLIAM TYNDALE —

From his treatise on the Lord's Prayer

9. *Our Father, who art in heaven*

LUKE 15:18

Our Father, who art in heaven,
what a great space there is between you and us.
Therefore, how shall we, your children here on earth,
banished and exiled from you in this valley of sadness and
  suffering,
come home to you,
into the true country of our birth?

10. *Hallowed be thy name*

PSALM 115:1

Father, it is only right for us to acknowledge our sin and
   trespass.
Be a merciful Father, and do not deal with us according to
   what we deserve,
nor judge us too rigorously,
but give us grace that we may live in such a way
that your holy name may be hallowed and sanctified in us.
Guard our hearts, so that we neither do nor speak—
in fact, that we neither think nor intend—
anything but that which will bring you honor and praise.
Above all things, may we seek the honor and glory of your
   name,
and not our own.
By your great power, bring us, your children,
to love and revere you as our heavenly Father. Amen.

11. *Thy kingdom come*

COLOSSIANS 1:13

O Father, we feel ourselves—
our hearts as well as our bodies—
prone and ready to sin.
The world, the flesh, and the devil seek to rule in us,
and to expel the honor that is due to your holy name.
Therefore, we pray, most merciful Father,
for the sake of the love you have for your only Son, Jesus
    Christ,
deliver us from this terrible bondage.
May your kingdom come—
to drive out the sin,
to loose the bonds of Satan,
to tame the flesh,
and to make us righteous and pure.
May we hold fast to you, so that you alone may reign in us,
that we may be your kingdom and possession
and obey you with all the power and strength of our hearts
    and bodies. Amen.

12. *Thy will be done, on earth as it is in heaven*

1 JOHN 2:17

Dear Father, open our eyes and work patience in us,
that we may understand the works of your hand,
and also patiently allow your will to be fulfilled in us.
Even though your strongest cure may be painful for us to
    bear,
still go on with it.
Do whatever is necessary for your will, and only yours, to
    be fulfilled.
And forbid us, Father, from following our own plans and
    imaginations,
from acting according to our own will, meaning, and
    purpose.
For your will and ours are often entirely contrary to one
    another—
yours being good and ours being flawed—
though in our blindness we usually see it the other way
    around. Amen.

13. *Give us this day our daily bread, and forgive us our trespasses, as we forgive those who trespass against us*

JOHN 6:33-34

Father, have mercy on us,

and do not withhold from us the daily bread of love.

It grieves us to the depths of our hearts

that we cannot follow your will in all things.

Please have patience with us, your wayward children.

Forgive our sin and guilt, and do not judge us according to
your righteous law,

for no one can be righteous in your presence.

Instead, remember your promise of forgiveness to those
who,

with all their hearts,

forgive those who trespass against them.

Of course, we cannot earn your forgiveness by forgiving
others,

but you are true to your word.

In your grace and mercy you have promised forgiveness

to all those who forgive their neighbors.

In this promise, therefore, we put all our hope and trust.

Amen.

14. *And lead us not into temptation, but deliver us from evil*

PSALM 70:1

Father, you know how much temptation comes
in times of adversity, suffering, pain, and evil.
Deliver us from them all.
Finish your healing work in us and make us thoroughly
    whole.
Then, set free from sin and evil,
may we be the kingdom of your own people,
to praise, honor, and worship you all our days.
You have taught us to pray this prayer,
and promised to hear us when we do.
So we hope in your mercy and trust that you will grant our
    requests.
May your word of truth be upheld and honored, now and
    forever. Amen.

MARTIN LUTHER

15. *Morning prayer*

PSALM 31:5

In the name of the Father, and of the Son, and of the Holy
 Spirit.
I thank you, my heavenly Father,
through Jesus Christ, your dear Son,
that you have kept me this night from all harm and danger;
and I pray that you would keep me this day also from sin
 and every evil,
that all my doings and life may please you.
For into your hands I commend myself,
my body and soul,
and all things.
Let your holy angel be with me,
that the evil foe may have no power over me. Amen.

16. *Evening Prayer*

PSALM 17:8

In the name of the Father, and of the Son, and of the Holy
   Spirit.

I thank you, my heavenly Father,

through Jesus Christ, your dear Son,

that you have graciously kept me this day;

I pray that you would forgive me all the sins and wrongs I
   have done,

and graciously keep me this night.

For into your hands I commend myself,

my body and soul,

and all things.

Let your holy angel be with me,

that the evil foe may have no power over me. Amen.

17. *A call for help*

JOHN 2:6-7

Behold, Lord, an empty vessel that needs to be filled. My
　　Lord, fill it.
I am weak in faith; strengthen me.
I am cold in love; warm me and make me fervent,
that my love may go out to my neighbor.
I do not have a strong and firm faith;
at times I doubt and am unable to trust you altogether.
O Lord, help me. Strengthen my faith and trust in you.
I have sealed the treasures of all I have in you.
I am poor; you are rich, and you came to be merciful to the
　　poor.
I am a sinner; you alone are true.
In me there is an abundance of sin; in you is the fullness of
　　righteousness.
Therefore, I will remain with you,
from whom I can receive,
but to whom I may not give.
Amen.

18. *Thanks and confidence*

COLOSSIANS 4:4-6

With heart and voice before the world,
I thank, praise, and glorify you, my Lord Christ,
that you are merciful to me and help me.
This I have received in baptism,
that you, and none other,
shall be my Lord and God. Amen.

19. *Thanksgiving for salvation*

ROMANS 8:1

O my God, I am a sinner, and yet I am not a sinner.

Alone and apart from Christ, I am a sinner.

But in my Lord Jesus Christ and with him, I am no sinner.

I firmly believe that he has destroyed all my sins with his
precious blood.

The sign of this is that I am baptized,

cleansed by God's word,

and declared absolved and freed from all my sins.

In the sacrament of the true body and blood of my Lord
Jesus Christ

I have received, as a sure sign of grace, the forgiveness of
sins.

This he has won and accomplished for me

by the shedding of his precious blood.

For this I thank him in eternity. Amen.

20. *To walk with God*

2 CORINTHIANS 12:9

Dear God and Father, I thank you for your infinite
goodness and love to me.
You continually keep me in your word, in faith, and in
prayer.
By this I know how to walk before you in humility and in
fear.
By this I am not proud of my own wisdom, righteousness,
skill, and strength,
but glory alone in your power.
You are strong when I am weak,
and through my weakness you win daily and gain the
victory. Amen.

21. *Make me a fruitful garden*

JOHN 15:16

Dear God and Father, I pray for you to so nurture me
that I may be to you as a beautiful garden,
so that many people may enjoy your fruit
and be attracted through me to all godliness.
Write into my heart, by your Holy Spirit,
whatever is abundantly found in Scripture.
Let me constantly keep your word in mind,
and permit it to become far more precious to me than my
    own life
and all else that I cherish on earth.
Help me to live and act accordingly.
To you be praise and thanks in eternity. Amen.

22. *When I am weak in doing good*

1 JOHN 2:15

Lord God, I have indeed transgressed your
  commandments.
I have been impatient in troubles and trials.
I am unsympathetic and unmerciful.
I do not help my neighbor.
I am unable to resist sin.
I do not tire of doing wrong.
Dear Lord, pour out your grace to me and give me your
  Holy Spirit
so that I may be obedient and keep each of your
  commandments.
Help me to be at odds with the world
and to give my heart and soul to you. Amen.

23. *For a heart at peace*

PHILIPPIANS 4:7

Dear God, give me a steady heart and a true courage in all
   my striving against the devil,
so that I may not only endure and finally triumph,
but also have peace in the midst of the struggle.
May I praise and thank you
and not complain or become impatient against your divine
   will.
Let peace win the victory in my heart, so that, in my
   impatience,
I will not initiate anything against you or my neighbor.
May I remain quiet and peaceable toward you and toward
   other people,
both inwardly and outwardly,
until the final and eternal peace shall come. Amen.

24. *For the Holy Spirit*

ACTS 2:38

Dear Father in heaven, for the sake of your dear Son, Jesus
  Christ,

grant me your Holy Spirit,

that I may be a true disciple of Christ,

and therefore acquire a heart with a never-ceasing fountain
  of love. Amen.

25. *Help me to forgive*

LUKE 6:37

Dear God, I have been wronged. Why?
I do not deserve it of this person.
But I must remember and understand who I am to you.
There is a long complaint against me,
proving that I am ten times worse
and have sinned a thousand times more against you
than my neighbor has against me.
Therefore I must agree with your wish by sincerely praying:
O Lord, forgive, and I will also forgive. Amen.

26. *Hear my complaint*

PSALM 41:9

My Lord Jesus Christ, my neighbor has injured me,

hurt my honor by talking about me, and interfered with my
rights.

I cannot tolerate this, and I wish to avoid any contact.

O God, hear my complaint.

I would gladly feel kindly toward my neighbor, but I
cannot.

How totally cold and insensible I am.

O Lord, I am helpless and forsaken.

If you change me, I will be sincere.

O dear God, change me by your grace, or I must remain as
I am. Amen.

27. *For faith in times of trouble*

JOHN 16:33

O Father and God of all comfort,

through your word and Holy Spirit

grant me a firm, glad, and grateful faith.

By such faith may I easily overcome this and every other
trial,

and at length realize that what your dear Son Jesus Christ
himself says is true:

"But take courage; I have conquered the world." Amen.

28. *Under the weight of responsibility*

1 PETER 5:7

Heavenly Father, you are indeed my Lord and God.
You have created me out of nothing
and have also redeemed me through your Son.
Now you have placed special responsibility upon me.
Here my will is not respected,
and there is so much that bothers and worries me,
for which I can find neither help nor counsel by myself.
Therefore let these cares become yours.
Grant me your help and counsel.
Be all things to me in this place. Amen.

29. *To bear my cross*

LUKE 22:42

Dear God, I am your child.
You have sent me a cross and suffering, saying to me:
Suffer a little for my sake and I will reward you well.
Dear God, because it is your will,
I will gladly suffer. Amen.

30. *For true understanding*

PSALM 25:4

Dear Lord God, give me your grace that I may rightly
   understand your Word,
and more than that, do it.
O most blessed Lord Jesus Christ,
see to it that my search after knowledge leads me to glorify
   you alone.
If not, let me not know a single letter.
Give only what I, a poor sinner, need to glorify you. Amen.

31. *For patience in adversity*

1 CORINTHIANS 1:3-4

O Father of all mercy and God of all comfort,
strengthen and uphold me by your Spirit.
You command that I should wait on you
until the reason for my trial shall appear.
For you take no pleasure in permitting me to suffer and be
grieved.
In fact, you do not permit any evil to be done
unless you can make it serve a good purpose.
You see my distress and weakness.
Therefore you will help and deliver me. Amen.

32. *For guidance*

PSALM 46:10

Dear heavenly Father, say something.
I will gladly remain silent and be a child and student.
If I ruled my life with my own knowledge, wisdom, and
understanding,
I would have been sunk long ago.
Therefore, dear God, you guide and direct it.
I will gladly forsake my point of view and understanding
and let you rule alone through your Word. Amen.

33. *When I feel helpless*

PSALM 127:1

Lord, what you do not do remains undone.
If you will not help, I will gladly surrender.
The cause is not mine.
I will happily be your mask and disguise,
if only you will do the work. Amen.

34. *For my family*

EPHESIANS 3:14–15

O Lord Jesus Christ, you have commanded me to love my
   wife (husband) faithfully,
and to bear the responsibilities of family life diligently and
   humbly.
I will gladly do this.
You have made me father (mother) of a family.
Dear Lord, make me a devout parent.
Help me to discharge my duties with heart and soul.
I would rather lose my life
than disobey you by offending my children and members
   of my household,
or by failing to guide them faithfully.
You will not permit this blessing of yours to be disturbed or
   destroyed,
but will graciously protect it through Jesus Christ our Lord.
   Amen.

35. *For steadfast faith*

JOHN 12:35

O God, what would I be if you were to forsake me?
What can I do if you withdraw your hand?
What can I know if you do not enlighten me?
How quickly the educated become infants;
the prudent, simple;
the wise, fools!
How awesome you are in all your works and judgments!
Let me walk in the light while I have light,
so that I may not be caught in darkness.
Many renounce their faith and become careless and weary
  in your grace.
They are deceived into thinking they know everything and
  have no need.
They feel satisfied and become slothful and ungrateful and
  are soon ruined.
Therefore help me to remain in the fervor of faith,
that I may daily increase in it through Jesus Christ,
my real and only helper. Amen.

36. *For my daily needs*

PSALM 42:11

Dear Father, give, I pray, daily bread, good seasons, and
    health.
Protect me from violence, sickness, and disaster.
If you would test me a bit by withholding your blessings for
    a while,
then your will be done.
If my time is up and my hour has come,
deliver me from all evil.
If not, give me strength and patience. Amen.

37. *I am yours*

ROMANS 14:8

O Jesus Christ, I live to you;
I die to you;
living or dying,
I am yours. Amen.

38. *The Good Shepherd*

JOHN 10:11

My Lord Jesus Christ, you are indeed the only Shepherd,
and I, sorry to say, am the lost and straying sheep.
I am anxious and afraid.
Gladly would I be devout and cling to you, my gracious
  God,
and so have peace in my heart.
I learn that you are as anxious for me as I am for you.
I am eager to know how I can come to you for help.
Anxiously you desire above all else to bring me back to
  yourself again.
Then come to me.
Seek and find me.
Help me also to come to you,
and praise and honor you forever. Amen.

39. *All that I have is yours*

1 CHRONICLES 29:14

O Lord, come to me
and use my bread, silver, and gold.
How very well they are spent
if I spend them in your service. Amen.

40. *For trust in God for everything*

MATTHEW 6:25

Dear God, why should I be anxious and worry about my
　　body and its food?

How do you raise up the grain in the field and all the fruits?

The world with all its wisdom and power is not able to
　　make a stalk, a tiny leaf, or a flower.

In you I have a Lord who can multiply one loaf as much as
　　you please,

without the aid of a farmer, a miller, or a baker.

As you do this day by day,

why should I worry whether you can or will supply my
　　needs?

— MARTIN BUCER —

41. *For the making of true disciples*

PSALM 119:1-2

Eternal God, gracious Father:
your will is that we work together to create places among
    your people
in which your word and teaching may be preserved and
    spread.
Grant us your help, who are gathered here in your name,
so that all we say or do may serve to make your glory
    known
and contribute to the good of your church.
Through your Son, our Savior Jesus Christ,
who lives and reigns with you in the unity of the Holy
    Spirit,
forever and ever. Amen.

42. *My life is in God*

ACTS 17:28

Heavenly Father, hear the prayer I make before you.
Drive from my heart and soul all those things that
    displease you.
Enable me to understand
that I live and move and have my being in you;
and that my sins are so great and so offensive before you,
that neither your grace nor your life ever could have been
    restored to me
except through the death of your only Son, Jesus Christ, my
    Lord. Amen.

43. *For faith in the love of God*

JOHN 3:16

Heavenly Father, enable me to grasp by true faith
that you have such love for me,
that you gave your dear Son up to death for me,
so that when I believe in him
I will not perish, but have everlasting life. Amen.

44. *For love of God and neighbor*

MARK 12:29–31

Merciful God and Father,

draw my heart and soul to your Son,

so that I may receive such a love as his with living faith and
eternal gratitude,

and therefore die to all evil more and more each day,

grow and increase in all goodness,

and lead my life with respect, patience, and love toward my
neighbor.

Greatly comforted by your holy gospel,

I will now and always call upon you, my God and Father.
Amen.

45. *To walk in the light of Christ*

1 JOHN 1:7

Grant, O heavenly Father,
that the remembrance of my redemption may never leave
my heart,
but that I may walk in Christ, the Light of the world,
far removed from my own foolish reason and blind will,
which will only lead me into pride and harmful darkness.
Amen.

46. *For a life dedicated to God and others*

1 THESSALONIANS 3:12

Almighty God, heavenly Father,

I praise and thank you for being so gracious to me, a poor
   sinner.

You have drawn me to your Son, my Lord Jesus,

whom you delivered to death for me,

and who has become both my food and my home for
   eternal life.

Grant that my heart may never lose hold of these things,

but always grow and increase in such faith,

that, through love, it will show forth in good works.

May my whole life be devoted to your praise

and to the good of my neighbor;

through the same Jesus Christ, your Son. Amen.

THOMAS CRANMER

47. *Thanksgiving at mealtime*

PSALM 34:8

Lord Jesus Christ, without you nothing is sweet or savory;
we ask you to bless us and our meal.
Cheer our hearts with your presence,
that in all our food and drink,
we may taste and enjoy you,
to your honor and glory. Amen.

48. *For willingness to bear my cross*

LUKE 9:23

Almighty God and Father,

your only and dearly beloved Son, our Savior Jesus Christ,

willingly suffered death and bitter pain for my redemption
and salvation.

Whenever you lay upon my back a similar cross and
affliction,

may I also, following his example, willingly and patiently
bear it,

as a true trial of my faith, and to your everlasting glory.

Hear my prayer, heavenly Father, for our Lord Jesus Christ's
sake. Amen.

49. *For the light of Christ*

JOHN 8:12

O Lord Jesus Christ, you are the bright sun of the world—
ever rising, never setting—
who with one look gives life:
preserving, nourishing, and making joyful all things that
   are in heaven and on earth.
Shine brightly, I pray, upon my heart,
that the darkness of sin may be driven away by your inward
   light,
and that I, without stumbling or offending you in any way,
may walk in the pure light of day all my life.
Grant this, O Lord, for with the Father and the Holy Spirit
you live and reign for evermore. Amen.

50. *A prayer before sleep*

PSALM 55:22

O Lord God, gracious and merciful,
you instruct me to cast out fear and care from my heart,
and to cast them on you,
promising most mercifully to be my protector from all my
    enemies,
my refuge in danger,
my guide through the day,
my light in the darkness,
and my watchman in the night.
You never sleep, but watch continually to preserve your
    faithful ones.
I pray that, in your bountiful goodness, O Lord,
you would forgive me for any way I have offended you this
    day,
and keep me under your protection through this night,
that I may rest in quietness,
in both body and soul. Amen.

51. *A prayer for the night*

PSALM 4:8

O Lord God, grant sleep to my eyes,
but let my heart keep perpetual watch with you.
So that the weakness of the flesh does not cause me to
   offend you, Lord,
let me at all times feel your goodness toward me.
At midday may your praise be in my mouth,
and at midnight, Lord, instruct me in your ways,
that all the course of my life may be led in holiness and
   purity,
until I enter at last into the everlasting rest
which you have promised, by your mercy,
to all who obey your word.
To you, O Lord, be honor, praise, and glory forever. Amen.

52. *Send me your Holy Spirit*

1 CORINTHIANS 13:3

Lord God, you have taught me that anything I do without
   love is worth nothing,
for whoever lives without love is counted dead before you.
Send your Holy Spirit,
and pour into my heart that most excellent gift of love,
which is the true bond of peace and of all virtues.
Grant this for the sake of your Son Jesus Christ,
who is alive with you and the Holy Spirit,
one God now and forever. Amen.

53. *To die and rise with Christ*

COLOSSIANS 3:3

O God, for my redemption you gave your only begotten
　　Son to the death of the Cross,
and by his glorious resurrection you delivered me from the
　　power of my enemy:
Grant me so to die daily from sin,
that I may evermore live with him in the joys of his
　　resurrection,
through the same Christ our Lord. Amen.

54. *I can do nothing without you, Lord*

JOHN 15:5

Grant, Lord, I pray,
the spirit always to think and do the things that are true,
that I, who can do nothing without you,
may be able to live according to your will,
through Jesus Christ our Lord. Amen.

PHILIP MELANCHTHON

55. *A morning prayer*

PSALM 88:13

Almighty, eternal God, Father of our Lord Jesus Christ,
  Creator of heaven and earth, and all humanity,
  together with your Son, our Lord Jesus Christ, your word
  and image,
  and with your Holy Spirit:
have mercy upon me,
  and forgive my sins for your Son's sake,
  whom you have made our Mediator according to your
  wonderful counsels;
  and guide and sanctify me by your Holy Spirit,
  which was poured out upon the Apostles.
  Grant that I may truly know and praise you throughout
  all eternity! Amen.

56. *For others*

JOHN 17:21

To you, O Son of God, Lord Jesus Christ,
as you pray to the eternal Father,
I pray, make us one in him.
Lighten our personal distress, and that of our society.
Receive us into the fellowship of those who believe.
Turn our hearts, O Christ, to everlasting truth and healing
    harmony. Amen.

57. *To begin the day*

ROMANS 13:12

I give most hearty thanks to you, O heavenly Father,
through your dear Son Jesus Christ,
that through this past night you, in your fatherly goodness,
have preserved me from all evil, and given my body rest
  and sleep.
Now I ask that, as you have raised up my body from sleep,
you will likewise deliver my mind from the sleep of sin,
and from the darkness of this world,
that walking in the light of your blessed Word,
I may do only that which is pleasing in your sight,
profitable to my neighbor,
and healthful to my soul. Amen.

58. *A Prayer to My Redeemer*

ROMANS 8:33

Almighty, Eternal God of Truth, I confess,
and I am deeply sorry,
that I am sinful and have so often sinned against you.
I implore you to forgive me all my sins,
be gracious to me,
and justify me for the sake of your beloved Son,
whom you have made my Redeemer.
With your Holy Spirit purify my heart and guide my soul
that I may truly know, adore, and be obedient you,
O God of Truth, Eternal Father, Son, and Holy Spirit.
  Amen.

59. *For God's mercy and forgiveness*

LUKE 18:38

Almighty and ever-living God of Truth,
Maker of heaven and earth, and Creator of all humanity,
together with your eternal beloved Son, our Lord Jesus
  Christ,
who was crucified for me and raised from death,
and with your Holy Spirit, ever-living, pure and true:
O God of wisdom and goodness, mercy and justice:
O Savior bountiful, righteous, and faithful,
through whom life and light are given: You have said,
"I do not desire the death of sinners, but that they be
  converted and live," and
"Call on me in time of trouble, and I will deliver you."
I confess myself a miserable sinner, burdened with many
  iniquities.
I have sinned against your holy commands
and I am heartily sorry for offending you.
For the sake of your dear Son,
have mercy on me and forgive me all my sins.

Make me righteous through Jesus Christ, my Lord,
your eternal Image and Word,
for you sent him into the world to be for me
a Sacrifice, Mediator, Redeemer, Deliverer, and Savior.
And all this is according to your wondrous wisdom and
    mercy,
which far surpasses my understanding. Amen.

60. *Sanctify me, O Lord*

PSALM 25:2

Almighty God, sanctify me with your holy, living Spirit of
   purity and truth,

that through your Spirit I may truly know you as the only
   God,

the omnipotent Creator of heaven and earth,

the Father of our Lord Jesus Christ;

that I may know your Holy Spirit of truth and purity, my
   living Comforter;

that I may firmly believe in you,

obey you,

give thanks to you,

reverently fear and call upon you,

and come at last in joy to behold your face and worship you
   forever.

In you, O Lord, I put my trust; let me never be ashamed.

Deliver me through your righteousness.

Turn me, O Lord, to righteousness and eternal life

for you have redeemed me, O Lord God of Truth! Amen.

61. *For the country*
PSALM 33:12

Ever-living God, mercifully preserve and rule our churches,
  our country, our schools.

Give the blessings of peace and order.

Direct and protect our leaders and those in authority.

Gather to yourself and forever keep a Christian Church in
  this land.

Purify and unite us with your Holy Spirit,

that we may be one in you,

truly knowing and calling upon you through your Son, our
  Lord, Jesus Christ,

who tasted death on the cross for us and rose again. Amen.

62. *In you I trust, O Lord*

HEBREWS 7:25

Almighty, eternal Son of God, our Lord and Savior, Jesus
   Christ,
you are the eternal Word and Image of the father,
our Mediator and Redeemer,
who died for us and rose again:
With all my heart I give you thanks,
for you took upon yourself my own human nature and
   became my Deliverer.
You suffered pain, you died, and you rose again.
And now you intercede for me.
Look graciously upon me, I pray, and have mercy,
for I am alone and in need.
Through the Holy Spirit increase in me the light of faith
and help me to overcome my weakness.
Guide, protect, and make me pure.
In you I trust, O Lord; let me never be ashamed. Amen.

63. *A prayer to the Holy Spirit*

ACTS 1:8

Almighty, Holy Spirit of truth and purity, our living
    Comforter:
enlighten me, direct me, and sanctify me.
Strengthen the faith in my soul and heart,
and grant me a sincere trust.
Sustain and guide me
that I may dwell in the house of the Lord all the days of my
    life,
that I may see the will of the Lord,
that I may forever be in God's holy temple,
to give thanks to him with a joyful heart,
and, in the fellowship of his eternal church,
to honor and praise him forever. Amen.

JOHN CALVIN

64. *A prayer for the new day*

PSALM 143:8

My God, my Father and my Savior,
you have been pleased to preserve me by your grace
    through the night
and you have brought me to this new day.
Grant that I may use it entirely in your service,
that I may think, say, and do nothing but to please you
and to obey your holy will.
May all my actions be to the glory of your name
and to the service of others.
And just as you cause the sun to shine on the world to give
    physical light,
let your Holy Spirit illumine my mind to guide me in the
    way of righteousness.
In everything I do, let my goal and intention always be
to walk reverently and to honor and serve you,
relying only on your blessing for my well-being,
and undertaking only what is pleasing to you. Amen.

65. *For perseverance*

LUKE 9:62

Heavenly Father, I know that beginning well means little
    unless one perseveres.
So, I ask you to be my guide,
not only today but for all my life.
Increase your grace in me each day,
until you have brought me into full union with your Son,
    Jesus Christ our Lord,
who is the true Sun of our souls,
shining day and night forever. Amen.

66. *For a restful night*

PSALM 42:8

Lord God, you have made the night for us to rest,
and you have created the day for us to work.
I ask you to give my body a restful night,
and to grant that my soul may be lifted up to you
and my heart always filled with your love. Amen.

67. *A commendation for the night*

PSALM 16:7

Teach me, O God, to entrust all my cares to you
and constantly to remember your mercy,
so that my soul may also enjoy spiritual rest.
Let me not sleep too much, but let this night renew my
   strength,
so I may be more ready to serve you.
Be pleased to keep me pure in body and spirit,
preserving me from all temptations and all danger,
so that even my sleep may be given to the glory of your
   name. Amen.

68. *For mercy before I sleep*

PSALM 4:8

Lord God, since I have not spent this day
without offending you in several ways,
I, who am a poor sinner, make this request:
Grant, O God, that just as you hide all things in the
　shadows of the night,
you will also bury my sins in your mercy,
through Jesus Christ my Savior. Amen.

69. *Before receiving Holy Communion*

1 CORINTHIANS 10:16

O God, in your fatherly goodness, you invite me today to
    receive these holy signs
of my peace and reconciliation with you,
and your Son, Jesus, who died for us, calls me to himself
as he calls all who are weary and carry heavy burdens.
You will surely not reject your servant who prays for grace
and seeks salvation and life in the death of Jesus Christ.
Now, therefore, lift my heart to you; give me your Holy
    Spirit.
Let me approach this table with humble repentance
and a thirsty soul that longs for your grace.
Strengthen my faith so that,
as I receive these visible signs in my hand,
I may receive by faith the broken body of Jesus Christ
and his blood shed for me,
as the nourishment of eternal life. Amen.

70. *For guidance on my earthly pilgrimage*

PSALM 119:102

Grant, Almighty God, since during my pilgrimage in this
world
I need the daily teaching and guidance of your Spirit,
that with true humility I may depend on your Word and
inward inspiration,
and not take too much on myself.
Grant, also, that I may be aware of my ignorance, blindness,
and stupidity,
and always flee to you,
never permitting myself to be drawn aside in any way
by the cunning of Satan or of ungodly voices.
May I remain so fixed in your truth that I never turn aside
from it,
while you direct me through the whole course of my
vocation.
Then, may I arrive at that heavenly glory that has been
obtained for us
through the blood of your only begotten Son. Amen.

71. *For true obedience and humility*

PSALM 139:23-24

Almighty God, not only did you create me,
but when you placed me in this world
you also enriched me with an abundance of blessings.
Grant that I may never transfer to others the glory that is
    due only to you.
May I never resist you with an iron hardness,
but render myself always pliable to you;
nor give myself up to my own devices,
but instead follow, with true obedience and humility,
the ways you have prescribed in your Word,
until at last, having put off whatever remains of my
    wrongful choices,
I may enjoy that blessed light you have prepared for me in
    heaven,
through Jesus Christ our Lord. Amen.

72. *For a life that bears spiritual fruit*

PSALM 92:12-13

Grant, Almighty God, that since you have kindly invited
　　me to come to you,
and have revealed your Word for my salvation—
O grant that I may willingly, and from the heart, obey you,
and become so teachable
that what you have designed for my salvation may not turn
　　to my destruction.
May that imperishable seed,
by which you have planted in me the hope of heavenly life,
so drive its roots into my heart and bring forth fruit,
that your name may be glorified.
And may I be so planted in the courts of your house
that I may grow and flourish,
and that fruit may appear through the whole course of my
　　life,
until at last I enjoy that blessed life that is laid up for me in
　　heaven,
through Christ our Lord. Amen.

73. *Make me careful and alert*

PSALM 23:6

Almighty God, while in a cheerful and quiet state, I call out
  to you.
Relying on your protection, may I live in safety.
At the same time make me careful and alert,
lest spiritual lethargy should creep over me,
and my mind and thought be drawn away from meditating
  on you.
Instead, may I so earnestly seek you, morning, evening,
  and at all times,
that I may advance through life toward the mark you have
  set before me,
until at last I reach that heavenly kingdom,
which Christ your Son has obtained for me by his own
  blood. Amen.

74. *For complete submission to God*

JAMES 4:7

Grant, Almighty God, that I may submit myself completely
   to you,
and from my heart render you obedience.
To this purpose may I apply all my efforts and direct all my
   doings,
so that, having finished the course of this life,
I may at length come into that blessed rest
that has been prepared for me in heaven by Christ our
   Lord. Amen.

75. *When I have fallen*

LAMENTATIONS 3:22–23

Almighty God, though daily I depart from you by my sins,

grant that I may never be wholly removed

from the foundation on which my salvation depends.

Sustain me, or even raise me up when I have fallen,

that I may continue in your ways and always return to you
in true repentance.

And whatever may happen to me, may I learn always to
look to you,

and never despair of your goodness,

which you have promised is firm and unending.

Finally and especially, while relying on your only begotten
Son, our mediator,

may I be able to call on you as my Father,

until I come at last to that eternal inheritance

which you have obtained for me by the blood of your only
Son. Amen.

76. *For perseverance*

HEBREWS 12:1–2

Grant, Almighty God, that I may remain entirely obedient
   to your Word,
and never bend aside from it in any way.
Instruct me by the unconquerable power of your Spirit.
May I never surrender to any human terrors or threats,
but persevere in honoring your name to the end of my
   days.
However the world may rage after its own diabolical errors,
may I never turn aside from the right path,
but continue on the course to which you have called me,
until, after finishing my race,
I arrive at that happy rest laid up for me in heaven,
through Christ our Lord. Amen.

77. *For guidance and protection*

LUKE 12:6-7

Grant, Omnipotent God,
that I may flee to you and resign myself wholly to your will;
that I may know that you are the guardian of my life;
and that not a hair on my head can fall without your
    permission.
May I also learn to ask you for the spirit of wisdom and
    discretion,
so that you may always guide my steps.
I am not able to defend myself
from the many deceptions that surround me on every side,
nor from the forces of the world that oppose me.
May I proceed on the course of my pilgrimage
under your care and protection,
until, removed from this earth,
I am taken into that blessed rest laid up for me in heaven
by Christ our Lord. Amen.

78. *For humility and simplicity*

2 CORINTHIANS 3:18

Grant, Almighty God,
since you have not only created me out of nothing,
but intend to create me again in your only begotten Son;
and since you have taken me from the lowest depths,
so that you may raise me to the hope of your heavenly
   kingdom:
Grant, I pray,
that I may not be proud or puffed up with conceit;
but may embrace your favor with humility,
and submit myself to you in simplicity,
until at last I become a partaker of that glory
your only begotten Son has acquired for me. Amen.

79. *Fixing my eyes on Christ*

HEBREWS 12:3

Grant, Almighty God,
since you have appeared in the person of your only
    begotten Son
and have revealed in him your glory made visible;
and, since you show us the same Christ through the
    window of the gospel:
Grant that I, fixing my eyes on him,
may not go astray, nor be led here and there after
evil lies, the misleadings of Satan, and the allurements of
    this world.
Instead, may I continue firm in the obedience of faith
and persevere in it through the whole course of my life,
until I am at last transformed into the image of your eternal
    glory,
which now in part shines in me,
through the same Christ our Lord. Amen.

80. *For readiness to follow God's calling*

2 TIMOTHY 1:6-7

O Lord, source of all wisdom and knowledge,
since it has pleased you to provide me during my youth
with the teaching I need to lead a holy and honest life,
enlighten my intelligence so that I may understand the
    instruction I have been given.
You have promised to enlighten the upright in heart who
    are little and humble,
while you reject the proud so they get lost in their own vain
    reasoning.
I ask you, O my God, to create in me the true humility
that will make me teachable and obedient,
first of all to you,
but also to those you have appointed to teach me.
Grant at the same time that, having renounced all evil
    desires,
my heart may fervently seek you,
and that my only goal, O God,
may be to prepare myself from this time forward
to serve you in the vocation to which you will call me.
    Amen.

81. *To hear God's voice in the morning*

PSALM 143:10

Grant that I may hear your voice in the morning, for my
hope is in you.

Show me the way in which I should walk, for I lift my soul
to you.

Deliver me from my enemies, O Lord, for I have fled to
you.

Teach me to do your will, for you are my God.

Let your good Spirit lead me in the right way. Amen.

82. *To aim for heavenly goals*

COLOSSIANS 3:1

O God, to whatever purpose I apply my mind today,
may my goal and intention be your honor and service.
May I expect happiness only from your goodness.
Let me not attempt anything, O God, that is not pleasing to
you.
Grant also, Lord,
that while I work to provide for this earthly life and its
concerns,
I may raise my mind above them to the blessed and
heavenly life,
which you have promised to your children. Amen.

83. *For God's protection*

PSALM 91:3-4

O God, show yourself to be my Protector,
to strengthen me against the assaults of the devil,
and to deliver me from all the dangers
that continually threaten me in this life. Amen.

84. *For God's forgiveness*

PSALM 145:18

O God, so that I may receive from you
all your great and manifold blessings,
please forget,
and in your infinite mercy, forgive my sins,
as you have promised you would
to all who call upon you with a sincere heart.
Through Jesus Christ our Savior. Amen.

85. *For remembrance of God's goodness*

PSALM 77:11

Let me never forget you, O Lord,
nor your goodness.
Let the remembrance of your mercy
be always engraved on my mind. Amen.

JOHN KNOX

86. *Thanksgiving at the close of the week*

EPHESIANS 5:20

Honor and praise be to you, O Lord, my God,
for all the tender mercies you have again given to me
through another week.
Continual thanks be to you for creating me in your own
likeness;
for redeeming me by the precious blood of your dear Son
when I was lost;
and for sanctifying me with the Holy Spirit.
For your help and support with my needs;
your protection in the many dangers of body and soul;
your comfort in my sorrows;
and for sparing me in life, and giving me so long a time to
repent.

For all these benefits, O most merciful Father,
that I have received by your goodness alone,
I thank you;
and I pray that you will always grant me your Holy Spirit,
so that I may grow in grace,
in steadfast faith,
and in perseverance in all good works,
through Jesus Christ my Lord. Amen.

87. *For all in Christ's flock*

HEBREWS 13:20–21

O God of all power,
you have called from death the great Shepherd of the sheep,
   our Lord Jesus:
Comfort and defend the flock which you have redeemed
by the blood of your eternal covenant;
increase the number of true pastors;
relieve and enlighten the hearts of the weak;
ease the pains of the afflicted,
and especially of those who suffer for their witness to the
   Truth,
by the power of our Lord Jesus Christ. Amen.

88. *For the fruitful planting of God's word*

MARK 4:20

Almighty God, and most merciful Father,
I humbly submit myself to you and bow down before your
　　majesty,
praying from the bottom of my heart that the seed of your
　　word,
which you have sown within me, may take such deep root,
that the burning heat of persecution may not cause it to
　　wither,
nor the thorny cares of this life choke it,
but that, as seed sown in good ground,
it may bring forth thirty, sixty, and a hundredfold,
according to the direction of your heavenly wisdom.
And, because I continually need to look for many things
　　from your hand,
I humbly ask for your Holy Spirit to direct my requests,
so that they may proceed from truthful intentions
that are in agreement with your most blessed will. Amen.

89. *For protection, from within and without*

1 JOHN 2:16-17

Increase my faith, O merciful Father,
that I may not swerve at any time from your heavenly
word.
Give me an increase of hope and love,
together with a careful keeping of all your commandments,
that no hardness of heart, no hypocrisy,
no lust of the eyes, nor any methods of the world,
may draw me away from obedience to you.
And, since we live now in these most perilous times,
let your fatherly providence defend me against all violence
and harm. Amen.

90. *For a thankful heart*

1 CORINTHIANS 1:9

Most merciful Father,
I give you all praise and thanks and glory,
for you have been pleased to give me, a miserable sinner,
so excellent a gift and treasure,
as to be received into the fellowship and company
of your dear Son Jesus Christ, my Lord.
I pray now that you would grant this request—
that you would never allow me to grow so callous as to
   forget your many blessings,
but rather, imprint and fix them firmly in my heart,
that I may grow and increase daily,
more and more,
in true faith. Amen.

THEODORE BEZA

91. *To be content in bearing my cross*

PHILIPPIANS 4:11

Grant, O Lord,

that I may attain the true wisdom that is always content
with your will,

which, for members of your household,

is none other than to bear my cross, after the example of
your Son.

Purge from me all lusts of the flesh,

and replenish within me the desires of eternal life.

May I learn in whatever state I am,

cheerfully to submit myself to the workings of your
wisdom,

being well assured, that whatever I suffer,

all the crosses of my life will be made blessings and helps
from you, my Father,

to make me go the right way into your kingdom,

and to increase in me the richness of your glory. Amen.

92. *I am yours, O God*

PSALM 16:2

I am always and forever yours, O God.
If you cast me out, who will take me in?
If you disregard me, who will consider me?
You forgive more sin than I can commit;
you have more mercy than I have offenses.
Do not let harmful pleasures overcome me;
at least do not let any perverse habit overwhelm me.
From evil and harmful desires;
from vain, cruel, and impure imaginations;
from the illusions of the devil and from dangers to my soul
   and body;
Good Lord, deliver me. Amen.

93. *When I read the Bible*

PSALM 51:15

O Lord, take away the veil of my heart while I read the
  Scriptures.
Blessed are you, O Lord:
O teach me your statutes!
Give me a word, O Word of the Father;
touch my heart;
enlighten the understandings of my mind;
open my lips,
and fill them with your praise. Amen.

94. *A prayer before meals*

PSALM 104:27–28

O God, you give food to all your creatures,
and feed even the young birds that cry out to you.
You have nourished us from our youngest days.
Fill our hearts with goodness and gladness,
and establish our hearts with your grace. Amen.

95. *Early in the morning*

PSALM 5:3

O Lord, you will hear my voice:
Early in the morning I will bring my prayer to you,
and will look up.
I remembered you in my bed,
and I thought about you when I was waking up,
because you have been my Helper.
I bring you thanks, Almighty Lord, everlasting God,
for you have preserved me through the night,
not according to my deserving, but according to your holy
   compassion.
Grant, O Lord,
that I may spend this day in your holy service,
that you will accept the gift of my obedience.
I lift up both my heart and my hands to the Lord in the
   heavens. Amen.

96. *Before sleep*

PSALM 65:8

Let me be mindful of your Name in the night, O Lord,
and keep your law.
Let my evening prayer ascend to you,
and your mercy descend to me;
You make the coming of the morning and the evening to
    praise you;
You give the ones you love the sleep of health. Amen.

97. *At the end of the day*

PSALM 90:12

O God, who has made the evening the end of the day,
so that you might bring the evening of life to my mind:
Grant me always to reflect that my life passes away like a
   day;
to remember the days of darkness, that they are many;
and that the night will come when no one can work.
Stay with me, O Lord,
for the evening draws near,
and this day of my life is now over. Amen.

98. *Deliver me, O Lord*

ISAIAH 57:15

Look down, O Lord, my God,
from the height of your dwelling place and from the throne
   of your glory.
You dwell on high, yet behold the humble:
Look down upon me and do not destroy;
rather, deliver me from evil.
From all evil and misfortune,
deliver me.
By whatever is dear to you or beloved by you,
deliver me.
In all my troubles,
deliver me. Amen.

99. *An act of thanksgiving*

PSALM 116:12

What shall I bring to the Lord for all the good things he has
    done for me?
What thanks can I give to God for all the joy with which I
    rejoice before him?
O Lord, you have appointed this holy day, and this hour,
for me to raise my mind to your praise,
And to offer you the glory due your Name.
O Lord, receive this spiritual sacrifice from my soul,
and, as you receive it at your spiritual altar,
be pleased,
in exchange,
to send me the grace of your most Holy Spirit. Amen.

100. *Before a journey*

EXODUS 33:15

Go before your servant this day, O Lord.
If you do not go with me yourself, then do not let me go.
You, who guided the Israelites by an angel,
the wise men by a star,
who preserved Peter in the waves,
and Paul in shipwreck:
Be present with me, O Lord, and order my way.
Go with me,
and lead me out,
and lead me back. Amen.

THE
REFORMATION
MICHAEL REEVES & JOHN STOTT

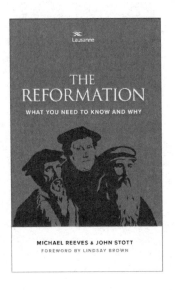

*The Reformation changed everything – culture,
commerce, and learning. In these few pages we focus on
its core, the apostolic teaching and courageous action
that defined a new Protestant church.
Here we have a fast-paced storyline of the whole period,
and a reflection on the part we must play in contending
for apostolic truth in our own times.*

ISBN 978-0-85721-874-2

E-ISBN 978-0-85721-875-9

THE
REFORMATION EXPERIENCE
ERIC IVES

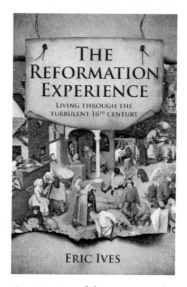

The Reformation was one of the most cataclysmic events in European history. But what was it really like to live through? How did ordinary people in England cope when some of their dearest beliefs were challenged, then reaffirmed, only to be challenged again? This book provides an important and gripping insight into the thoughts and lives of individual Englishmen and women.

ISBN 978-0-7459-5277-2

E-ISBN 978-0-7459-5889-7

The Reformation
Faith & Flames
ANDREW ATHERSTONE

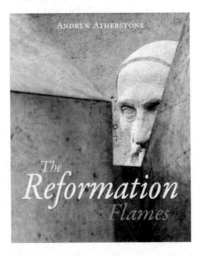

The reformation marked a period of profound upheaval – one of the greatest turning points in the history of Christianity – and sent shock waves through the western world. In this beautifully illustrated book, Andrew Atherstone traces the dramatic and compelling story. Focusing on the key personalities and events, he explains the often complex ideas that were at stake – and the political as well as religious issues involved. An authoritative account of a movement that changed the face of Europe forever.

ISBN: 978-0-7459-5305-2